Annie's BabyCakes

BabyCakes

Small Cheesecakes for Your Sweet Tooth

by Anne Yohn

Northland Publishing

Copyright © 1992 by Anne Yohn
All rights reserved.
This book may not be reproduced in whole or in part, by any means
(with the exception of short quotes for the purpose of review),
without permission of the publisher. For information, address
Northland Publishing Co., P.O. Box 1389, Flagstaff, Arizona 86002.
Designed by David Jenney

FIRST EDITION
ISBN 0-87358-535-6
Library of Congress Catalog Card Number 91-43002

Manufactured in the United States

Library of Congress Cataloging-in-Publication Data
Yohn, Anne.
Annie's BabyCakes : small cheesecakes for your sweet tooth /
by Anne Yohn. -- 1st ed.
72p.
ISBN 0-87358-535-6 (softcover) : $9.95
1. Cheesecake (Cookery)   I. Title. II. Title: BabyCakes.
TX773.Y66   1992   91-43002
641.8'653 -- dc20   CIP

3-92/5M/0382

Contents

Introduction 1

Preparation Hints 3

BAKED BABYCAKES 5

Amaretto 6
Apricot Brandy 7
Banana 8
Black Walnut and Kirsch 9
Blueberry-Lemon Surprise 10
Butterscotch 11
Cherry 12
Cherry-Chocolate 13
Chocolate Folly 14
Cosmopolitan 15
Grasshopper 16
Hazelnut 17
Key Lime 18
Lemon Zing 19
Maple Walnut 20
Mocha 21
Orange 22
Orange-Chocolate 23
Peach 24
Piña Colada 25
Pineapple 26
Pink Peppermint 27
Pomegranate-Tangerine 28
Raspberry 29
Rocky Road 30
Rose Petal 31
Tia Hanna's 32
Tiger Stripe 33
Tofu 34

Refrigerator BabyCakes 35

Almond-Chocolate 36
Amaretto 37
Apricot 38
Black Bottom 39
Black Forest 40
Blueberry 41
Brandy Alexander 42
Cherry 43
Chocolate 44
Chocolate-Hazelnut 45
Cosmopolitan 46
Eggnog 47
Ginger-Chocolate 48
Irish Cream 49
Lemon 50
Lime 51
Marble 52
Mocha 53
Orange 54
Peach 55
Pineapple 56
Strawberry 57
Turtle Walk 58

Toppings 59

Blueberry-Lemon Peel 60
Brandied Apricot 60
Butterscotch 61
Glazed Fresh Fruit 61
Grasshopper 61
Hazelnut 62
Jamaica Banana 62
Key Lime 63
Lemon Zing 63
Mango Melba 64
Marshmallow Meringue 64
Orange 65
Peach Melba 65

Introduction

CHEESECAKE IS A WONDERFULLY RICH DESSERT that is best served fresh. After many years of baking and serving cheesecakes to my family and friends, I began to wonder whether a smaller cheesecake might be the solution to leftovers.

I experimented by making smaller pans; my first were springform pans made from cardboard and aluminum foil, their sides fastened with pins. These pans served three to four people, but I still wasn't satisfied. I wanted to create a single-serving cheesecake.

One day while I was making tuna salad, I noticed the tuna can was the perfect shape and diameter for my cheesecakes. I tried a recipe using several of the cans, and the results were true miniature single-serving cheesecakes—Annie's BabyCakes were born.

The recipes in this book have been grouped into three sections. The first includes recipes for baked cheesecakes that are made from white or dark chocolates. You can make them quickly and easily. Alcoholic liqueurs are used in the recipes for flavoring, but you can easily substitute equal amounts of juices or other liquid flavorings if you wish. The second section contains recipes that require no baking at all. Both sections include quick topping suggestions with each recipe, and there are many more topping recipes in section three.

I hope you enjoy making these BabyCakes as much as I have. You will find them easy to prepare and attractive to serve—especially when grouped together on a large tray and decorated with fruits or other suggested toppings. Your guests will be quite impressed!

Preparation Hints

ANNIE'S BABYCAKES can be made as plain or as elaborate as you wish by varying the toppings. Each recipe makes four BabyCakes, which bake in far less time than full-sized cheesecakes (although you can make either with the recipes; for full-sized cheesecakes, double the recipe and bake for 35 to 40 minutes) and provide more variety for your family and guests. Bake the cakes in small three-inch pans: use food cans—the kind that tuna, chicken, water chestnuts, and other foods are packed in—or three-inch cake pans, which may be purchased from a specialty cake store. Annie's BabyCakes are small enough that you can invert the pans to remove the cheesecakes without damaging them.

Do not overbeat or overbake these cheesecakes. Overbeating introduces air, causing the BabyCakes to lose their creamy texture. Overbaking produces a dry BabyCake.

If you do not have the suggested crust ingredients on hand, use any kind of crushed dry cereals or cookies.

Most of the cheesecakes in the first section are not very sweet. If you prefer a sweeter cheesecake, add one to three tablespoons of sugar to the batter.

The baked BabyCakes are made with melted chocolates for smooth texture. Both white and dark chocolates can be melted in a double boiler or in the microwave. *Melt chocolates with caution.* White and dark chocolates quickly scorch if subjected to high-level heat. Using a double boiler of hot, not boiling, water is the safest method. Microwaving is quicker, but heat the chocolate carefully if you use this method. Since chocolate can

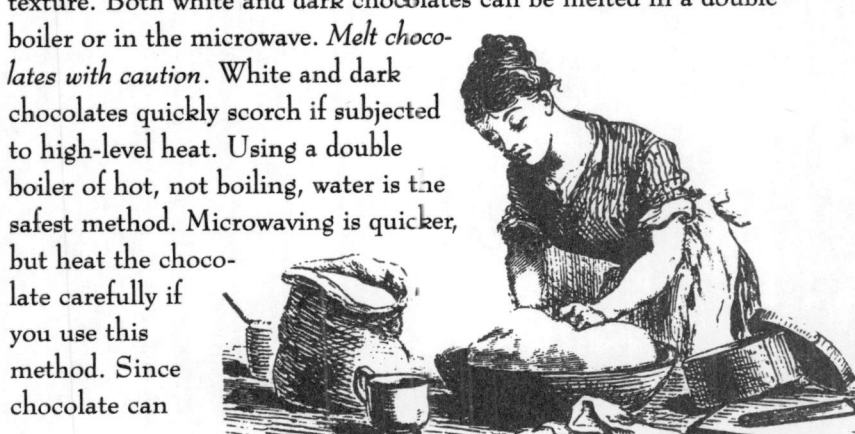

melt but still maintain its shape in the microwave, stir to check the degree of melting. Heat it at first for one minute on high. Stir and continue heating on medium low, checking the chocolate by stirring every fifteen seconds as it softens.

White chocolate is not really chocolate. The cocoa butter has been replaced with another vegetable fat, and the chocolate liqueur, which is the ingredient that actually provides the chocolate flavor, has been removed. White chocolate is often flavored and colored to make solid candies.

The liqueurs utilized in the recipes can be replaced by juices or other liquid flavorings if you wish. You can also substitute two to three egg whites for whole eggs. The volume measure of each recipe is about three cups, so if you make substitutions, be sure that they are approximately equal in volume to the original item.

The cheesecakes are better when prepared with the freshest ingredients. Make sure the cream cheese, sour cream, and eggs are fresh. Use real flavors if you can get them and fresh fruits for toppings.

At higher elevations (above 6,000 feet), you may need to use less liqueur and more cream cheese.

Have fun and be creative!

Baked BabyCakes

The recipes in this section require baking
(see page 35 for Refrigerator BabyCakes)
and use eggs as the setting agent.
Allow three hours preparation time,
because after baking (25 to 30 minutes)
the cheesecakes need to cool for an hour
and then chill in the refrigerator
for an hour before being served.

Amaretto BabyCake

Preheat oven to 325°. Place oven rack in center of oven.

CRUST

    4 3-inch pans
    1/3 stick margarine
    1 cup almond cake crumbs

Thinly spread bottom and sides of pans with margarine. Evenly coat bottom and sides of pans with crumbs and press into place. Save remaining crumbs for next use. Refrigerate pans while preparing batter.

BATTER (Ingredients must be at room temperature.)

    1 8-ounce package cream cheese
    1/4 cup sour cream
    1 egg, beaten
    1 cup melted white chocolate
    1/2 cup amaretto liqueur
    1 teaspoon almond flavoring

Beat cream cheese until smooth. Add sour cream and egg, mixing thoroughly. Quickly blend in melted chocolate and remaining ingredients. The batter may begin to stiffen as the chocolate cools.

    Pour equal portions of batter into the pans and bake at 325° for 25 to 30 minutes. To check, gently tap pans with flat of fingernail. Cakes are ready when edges are semiset and center still jiggles. DO NOT OVERBAKE. Baby-Cakes will continue to bake after they are removed from the oven.

    Remove BabyCakes from the oven and allow to cool about 1 hour, until they reach room temperature.

    Carefully run a smooth knife around the inside edges of each pan to loosen BabyCakes. Invert onto saucer, then onto dessert plate, crumb side down.

    Cover and refrigerate BabyCakes for at least 1 hour. Add desired topping just before serving. Serves 4.

SUGGESTED QUICK TOPPING
Serve plain, with powdered sugar, or with glazed fresh strawberries.

Apricot Brandy BabyCake

Preheat oven to 325°. Place oven rack in center of oven.

CRUST

    4 3-inch pans
    1/3 stick margarine
    1 cup vanilla cake crumbs

Thinly spread bottom and sides of pans with margarine. Evenly coat bottom and sides of pans with crumbs and press into place. Save remaining crumbs for next use. Refrigerate pans while preparing batter.

BATTER (Ingredients must be at room temperature.)

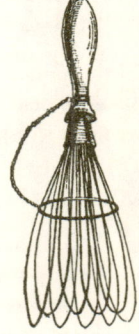

    1 8-ounce package cream cheese
    1/4 cup sour cream
    1 egg, beaten
    3/4 cup melted white chocolate
    Apricot-brandy mixture: Chop 4 dried apricot halves and soak in 1/2 cup apricot brandy (or apricot nectar) until plump. Drain off apricot brandy until mixture equals 2/3 cup.

Beat cream cheese until smooth. Add sour cream and egg, mixing thoroughly. Quickly blend in melted chocolate and remaining ingredients. The batter may begin to stiffen as the chocolate cools.

    Pour equal portions of batter into the pans and bake at 325° for 25 to 30 minutes. To check, gently tap pans with flat of fingernail. Cakes are ready when edges are semiset and center still jiggles. DO NOT OVERBAKE. Baby-Cakes will continue to bake after they are removed from the oven.

    Remove BabyCakes from the oven and allow to cool about 1 hour, until they reach room temperature.

    Carefully run a smooth knife around the inside edges of each pan to loosen BabyCakes. Invert onto saucer, then onto dessert plate, crumb side down.

    Cover and refrigerate BabyCakes for at least 1 hour. Add desired topping just before serving. Serves 4.

SUGGESTED QUICK TOPPING
Fresh or canned apricots glazed with warmed apricot jam or light corn syrup.

Banana BabyCake

Preheat oven to 325°. Place oven rack in center of oven.

CRUST

    4 3-inch pans
    $1/3$ stick margarine
    1 cup vanilla cake crumbs

Thinly spread bottom and sides of pans with margarine. Evenly coat bottom and sides of pans with crumbs and press into place. Save remaining crumbs for next use. Refrigerate pans while preparing batter.

BATTER (Ingredients must be at room temperature.)

    1 8-ounce package cream cheese
    $1/4$ cup sour cream
    1 egg, beaten
    $3/4$ cup melted white chocolate
    $1/2$ teaspoon nutmeg
    Banana-lemon juice mixture: Mash approximately $1/2$ ripe banana with 2 tablespoons lemon juice (amount should equal $2/3$ cup) and set aside.

Beat cream cheese until smooth. Add sour cream and egg, mixing thoroughly. Quickly blend in melted chocolate and remaining ingredients. The batter may begin to stiffen as the chocolate cools.

    Pour equal portions of batter into the pans and bake at 325° for 25 to 30 minutes. To check, gently tap pans with flat of fingernail. Cakes are ready when edges are semiset and center still jiggles. DO NOT OVERBAKE. Baby-Cakes will continue to bake after they are removed from the oven.

    Remove BabyCakes from the oven and allow to cool about 1 hour, until they reach room temperature.

    Carefully run a smooth knife around the inside edges of each pan to loosen BabyCakes. Invert onto saucer, then onto dessert plate, crumb side down.

    Cover and refrigerate BabyCakes for at least 1 hour. Add desired topping just before serving. Serves 4.

SUGGESTED QUICK TOPPING
Sliced bananas folded into sweetened whipped cream and sprinkled with nutmeg.

Black Walnut and Kirsch BabyCake

Preheat oven to 325°. Place oven rack in center of oven.

CRUST

   4 3-inch pans
   1/3 stick margarine
   1 cup chocolate cake crumbs

Thinly spread bottom and sides of pans with margarine. Evenly coat bottom and sides of pans with crumbs and press into place. Save remaining crumbs for next use. Refrigerate pans while preparing batter.

BATTER (Ingredients must be at room temperature.)

   1 8-ounce package cream cheese
   1/4 cup sour cream
   1 egg, beaten
   3/4 cup melted white chocolate
   1/3 cup maraschino cherry pieces
   1/3 cup ground black walnuts
   1/3 cup kirsch brandy

Beat cream cheese until smooth. Add sour cream and egg, mixing thoroughly. Quickly blend in melted chocolate and remaining ingredients. The batter may begin to stiffen as the chocolate cools.

Pour equal portions of batter into the pans and bake at 325° for 25 to 30 minutes. To check, gently tap pans with flat of fingernail. Cakes are ready when edges are semiset and center still jiggles. DO NOT OVERBAKE. BabyCakes will continue to bake after they are removed from the oven.

Remove BabyCakes from the oven and allow to cool about 1 hour, until they reach room temperature.

Carefully run a smooth knife around the inside edges of each pan to loosen BabyCakes. Invert onto saucer, then onto dessert plate, crumb side down.

Cover and refrigerate BabyCakes for at least 1 hour. Add desired topping just before serving. Serves 4.

SUGGESTED QUICK TOPPING

Sweetened whipped cream mixed with ground black walnuts and drained maraschino cherry pieces.

Blueberry-Lemon Surprise BabyCake

Preheat oven to 325°. Place oven rack in center of oven.

CRUST

    4 3-inch pans
    1/3 stick margarine
    1 cup vanilla wafer crumbs

Thinly spread bottom and sides of pans with margarine. Evenly coat bottom and sides of pans with crumbs and press into place. Save remaining crumbs for next use. Refrigerate pans while preparing batter.

BATTER (Ingredients must be at room temperature.)

    1 8-ounce package cream cheese
    1/4 cup sour cream
    1 egg, beaten
    3/4 cup melted white chocolate
    1 tablespoon grated lemon peel
    2/3 cup blueberry pie filling
    1 tablespoon lemon juice

Beat cream cheese until smooth. Add sour cream and egg, mixing thoroughly. Quickly blend in melted chocolate and remaining ingredients. The batter may begin to stiffen as the chocolate cools.

    Pour equal portions of batter into the pans and bake at 325° for 25 to 30 minutes. To check, gently tap pans with flat of fingernail. Cakes are ready when edges are semiset and center still jiggles. DO NOT OVERBAKE. BabyCakes will continue to bake after they are removed from the oven.

    Remove BabyCakes from the oven and allow to cool about 1 hour, until they reach room temperature.

    Carefully run a smooth knife around the inside edges of each pan to loosen BabyCakes. Invert onto saucer, then onto dessert plate, crumb side down.

    Cover and refrigerate BabyCakes for at least 1 hour. Add desired topping just before serving. Serves 4.

SUGGESTED QUICK TOPPING
Glazed blueberries. Decorate with lemon slices.

Butterscotch BabyCake

Preheat oven to 325°. Place oven rack in center of oven.

CRUST

    4 3-inch pans
    1/3 stick margarine
    1 cup finely ground pecans

Thinly spread bottom and sides of pans with margarine. Evenly coat bottom and sides of pans with nuts and press into place. Save remaining nuts for topping. Refrigerate pans while preparing batter.

BATTER (Ingredients must be at room temperature.)

    1 8-ounce package cream cheese
    1/2 cup sour cream
    1 egg, beaten
    3/4 cup melted butterscotch bits
    1/2 cup cooked butterscotch pudding
    1 teaspoon vanilla

Beat cream cheese until smooth. Add sour cream and egg, mixing thoroughly. Quickly blend in melted butterscotch bits and remaining ingredients. The batter may begin to stiffen as the butterscotch cools.

    Pour equal portions of batter into the pans and bake at 325° for 25 to 30 minutes. To check, gently tap pans with flat of fingernail. Cakes are ready when edges are semiset and center still jiggles. DO NOT OVERBAKE. Baby-Cakes will continue to bake after they are removed from the oven.

    Remove BabyCakes from the oven and allow to cool about 1 hour, until they reach room temperature.

    Carefully run a smooth knife around the inside edges of each pan to loosen BabyCakes. Invert onto saucer, then onto dessert plate, crumb side down.

    Cover and refrigerate BabyCakes for at least 1 hour. Add desired topping just before serving. Serves 4.

SUGGESTED QUICK TOPPING
Plain or whipped cream sprinkled with pecan bits.

Cherry BabyCake

Preheat oven to 325°. Place oven rack in center of oven.

CRUST

    4 3-inch pans
    1/3 stick margarine
    1 cup vanilla cake crumbs

Thinly spread bottom and sides of pans with margarine. Evenly coat bottom and sides of pans with crumbs and press into place. Save remaining crumbs for next use. Refrigerate pans while preparing batter.

BATTER (Ingredients must be at room temperature.)

    1 8-ounce package cream cheese
    1/4 cup sour cream
    1 egg, beaten
    3/4 cup melted white chocolate
    3/4 cup maraschino cherry pieces

Beat cream cheese until smooth. Add sour cream and egg, mixing thoroughly. Quickly blend in melted chocolate and remaining ingredients. The batter may begin to stiffen as the chocolate cools.

    Pour equal portions of batter into the pans and bake at 325° for 25 to 30 minutes. To check, gently tap pans with flat of fingernail. Cakes are ready when edges are semiset and center still jiggles. DO NOT OVERBAKE. Baby-Cakes will continue to bake after they are removed from the oven.

    Remove BabyCakes from the oven and allow to cool about 1 hour, until they reach room temperature.

    Carefully run a smooth knife around the inside edges of each pan to loosen BabyCakes. Invert onto saucer, then onto dessert plate, crumb side down.

    Cover and refrigerate BabyCakes for at least 1 hour. Add desired topping just before serving. Serves 4.

SUGGESTED QUICK TOPPING

Drained maraschino cherry pieces folded into sweetened whipped cream.

Cherry-Chocolate BabyCake

Preheat oven to 325°. Place oven rack in center of oven.

CRUST

    4 3-inch pans
    1/3 stick margarine
    1 cup chocolate cake crumbs

Thinly spread bottom and sides of pans with margarine. Evenly coat bottom and sides of pans with crumbs and press into place. Save remaining crumbs for next use. Refrigerate pans while preparing batter.

BATTER (Ingredients must be at room temperature.)

    1 8-ounce package cream cheese
    1/4 cup sour cream
    1 egg, beaten
    3/4 cup melted semisweet chocolate
    1 tablespoon cocoa
    1/4 cup maraschino cherry juice
    1/4 cup maraschino cherry pieces

Beat cream cheese until smooth. Add sour cream and egg, mixing thoroughly. Quickly blend in melted chocolate and remaining ingredients. The batter may begin to stiffen as the chocolate cools.

    Pour equal portions of batter into the pans and bake at 325° for 25 to 30 minutes. To check, gently tap pans with flat of fingernail. Cakes are ready when edges are semiset and center still jiggles. DO NOT OVERBAKE. BabyCakes will continue to bake after they are removed from the oven.

    Remove BabyCakes from the oven and allow to cool about 1 hour, until they reach room temperature.

    Carefully run a smooth knife around the inside edges of each pan to loosen BabyCakes. Invert onto saucer, then onto dessert plate, crumb side down.

    Cover and refrigerate BabyCakes for at least 1 hour. Add desired topping just before serving. Serves 4.

SUGGESTED QUICK TOPPING
Plain or sweetened whipped chocolate cream.

Chocolate Folly BabyCake

Preheat oven to 325°. Place oven rack in center of oven.

CRUST

    4 3-inch pans
    $1/3$ stick margarine
    1 cup chocolate cake crumbs

Thinly spread bottom and sides of pans with margarine. Evenly coat bottom and sides of pans with crumbs and press into place. Save remaining crumbs for next use. Refrigerate pans while preparing batter.

BATTER (Ingredients must be at room temperature.)

    1 8-ounce package cream cheese
    $1/2$ cup sour cream
    1 egg, beaten
    1 cup melted semisweet chocolate
    2 ounces melted margarine
    1 tablespoon cocoa powder

Beat cream cheese until smooth. Add sour cream and egg, mixing thoroughly. Quickly blend in melted chocolate and remaining ingredients. The batter may begin to stiffen as the chocolate cools.

Pour equal portions of batter into the pans and bake at 325° for 25 to 30 minutes. To check, gently tap pans with flat of fingernail. Cakes are ready when edges are semiset and center still jiggles. DO NOT OVERBAKE. BabyCakes will continue to bake after they are removed from the oven.

Remove BabyCakes from the oven and allow to cool about 1 hour, until they reach room temperature.

Carefully run a smooth knife around the inside edges of each pan to loosen BabyCakes. Invert onto saucer, then onto dessert plate, crumb side down.

Cover and refrigerate BabyCakes for at least 1 hour. Add desired topping just before serving. Serves 4.

SUGGESTED QUICK TOPPING
Strawberries and/or kiwi fruit and a dollop of whipped cream.

Cosmopolitan BabyCake

Preheat oven to 325°. Place oven rack in center of oven.

CRUST

    4 3-inch pans
    1/3 stick margarine
    1 cup vanilla cake crumbs

Thinly spread bottom and sides of pans with margarine. Evenly coat bottom and sides of pans with crumbs and press into place. Save remaining crumbs for next use. Refrigerate pans while preparing batter.

BATTER (Ingredients must be at room temperature.)

    1 8-ounce package cream cheese
    1/2 cup sour cream
    1 egg, beaten
    1 cup melted white chocolate
    1 teaspoon vanilla
    2 tablespoons lemon juice
    1 tablespoon grated orange peel

Beat cream cheese until smooth. Add sour cream and egg, mixing thoroughly. Quickly blend in melted chocolate and remaining ingredients. The batter may begin to stiffen as the chocolate cools.

    Pour equal portions of batter into the pans and bake at 325° for 25 to 30 minutes. To check, gently tap pans with flat of fingernail. Cakes are ready when edges are semiset and center still jiggles. DO NOT OVERBAKE. BabyCakes will continue to bake after they are removed from the oven.

    Remove BabyCakes from the oven and allow to cool about 1 hour, until they reach room temperature.

    Carefully run a smooth knife around the inside edges of each pan to loosen BabyCakes. Invert onto saucer, then onto dessert plate, crumb side down.

    Cover and refrigerate BabyCakes for at least 1 hour. Add desired topping just before serving. Serves 4.

SUGGESTED QUICK TOPPING
Whipped cream and sliced fruit.

Grasshopper BabyCake

Preheat oven to 325°. Place oven rack in center of oven.

CRUST

    4 3-inch pans
    1/3 stick margarine
    1 cup chocolate cake crumbs

Thinly spread bottom and sides of pans with margarine. Evenly coat bottom and sides of pans with crumbs and press into place. Save remaining crumbs for next use. Refrigerate pans while preparing batter.

BATTER (Ingredients must be at room temperature.)

    1 8-ounce package cream cheese
    1/4 cup sour cream
    1 egg, beaten
    1 cup melted white chocolate
    1/3 cup green creme de menthe
    1/3 cup white creme de cacao
    1 teaspoon chocolate flavoring

Beat cream cheese until smooth. Add sour cream and egg, mixing thoroughly. Quickly blend in melted chocolate and remaining ingredients. The batter may begin to stiffen as the chocolate cools.

Pour equal portions of batter into the pans and bake at 325° for 25 to 30 minutes. To check, gently tap pans with flat of fingernail. Cakes are ready when edges are semiset and center still jiggles. DO NOT OVERBAKE. BabyCakes will continue to bake after they are removed from the oven.

Remove BabyCakes from the oven and allow to cool about 1 hour, until they reach room temperature.

Carefully run a smooth knife around the inside edges of each pan to loosen BabyCakes. Invert onto saucer, then onto dessert plate, crumb side down.

Cover and refrigerate BabyCakes for at least 1 hour. Add desired topping just before serving. Serves 4.

SUGGESTED QUICK TOPPING
Whipped cream drizzled with chocolate syrup.

Hazelnut BabyCake

Preheat oven to 325°. Place oven rack in center of oven.

CRUST

    4 3-inch pans
    1/3 stick margarine
    1 cup finely ground hazelnuts

Thinly spread bottom and sides of pans with margarine. Evenly coat bottom and sides of pans with nuts and press into place. Save remaining nuts for topping. Refrigerate pans while preparing batter.

BATTER (Ingredients must be at room temperature.)

    1 8-ounce package cream cheese
    1/4 cup sour cream
    1 egg, beaten
    3/4 cup melted white chocolate
    1/3 cup finely ground hazelnuts
    1/3 cup Frangelica liqueur

Beat cream cheese until smooth. Add sour cream and egg, mixing thoroughly. Quickly blend in melted chocolate and remaining ingredients. The batter may begin to stiffen as the chocolate cools.

    Pour equal portions of batter into the pans and bake at 325° for 25 to 30 minutes. To check, gently tap pans with flat of fingernail. Cakes are ready when edges are semiset and center still jiggles. DO NOT OVERBAKE. BabyCakes will continue to bake after they are removed from the oven.

    Remove BabyCakes from the oven and allow to cool about 1 hour, until they reach room temperature.

    Carefully run a smooth knife around the inside edges of each pan to loosen BabyCakes. Invert onto saucer, then onto dessert plate, crumb side down.

    Cover and refrigerate BabyCakes for at least 1 hour. Add desired topping just before serving. Serves 4.

SUGGESTED QUICK TOPPING
Whipped cream sprinkled with ground hazelnuts.

Key Lime BabyCake

Preheat oven to 325°. Place oven rack in center of oven.

CRUST

 4 3-inch pans
 1/3 stick margarine
 1 cup vanilla cake crumbs

Thinly spread bottom and sides of pans with margarine. Evenly coat bottom and sides of pans with crumbs and press into place. Save remaining crumbs for next use. Refrigerate pans while preparing batter.

BATTER (Ingredients must be at room temperature.)

 1 8-ounce package cream cheese
 1/4 cup sour cream
 1 egg, beaten
 3/4 cup melted white chocolate
 2 tablespoons lime juice
 1 tablespoon grated lime peel
 1/2 cup warm lime Jello

Beat cream cheese until smooth. Add sour cream and egg, mixing thoroughly. Quickly blend in melted chocolate and remaining ingredients. The batter may begin to stiffen as the chocolate cools.

Pour equal portions of batter into the pans and bake at 325° for 25 to 30 minutes. To check, gently tap pans with flat of fingernail. Cakes are ready when edges are semiset and center still jiggles. DO NOT OVERBAKE. Baby-Cakes will continue to bake after they are removed from the oven.

Remove BabyCakes from the oven and allow to cool about 1 hour, until they reach room temperature.

Carefully run a smooth knife around the inside edges of each pan to loosen BabyCakes. Invert onto saucer, then onto dessert plate, crumb side down.

Cover and refrigerate BabyCakes for at least 1 hour. Add desired topping just before serving. Serves 4.

SUGGESTED QUICK TOPPING
Whipped cream and sliced star fruit.

Lemon Zing BabyCake

Preheat oven to 325°. Place oven rack in center of oven.

CRUST

    4 3-inch pans
    1/3 stick margarine
    1 cup vanilla cake crumbs

Thinly spread bottom and sides of pans with margarine. Evenly coat bottom and sides of pans with crumbs and press into place. Save remaining crumbs for next use. Refrigerate pans while preparing batter.

BATTER (Ingredients must be at room temperature.)

    1 8-ounce package cream cheese
    1/4 cup sour cream
    1 egg, beaten
    3/4 cup melted white chocolate
    1 tablespoon lemon juice
    1 tablespoon grated lemon peel
    1/2 cup warm lemon Jello

Beat cream cheese until smooth. Add sour cream and egg, mixing thoroughly. Quickly blend in melted chocolate and remaining ingredients. The batter may begin to stiffen as the chocolate cools.

    Pour equal portions of batter into the pans and bake at 325° for 25 to 30 minutes. To check, gently tap pans with flat of fingernail. Cakes are ready when edges are semiset and center still jiggles. DO NOT OVERBAKE. BabyCakes will continue baking after removal from oven.

    Remove BabyCakes from the oven and allow to cool about 1 hour, until they reach room temperature.

    Carefully run a smooth knife around the inside edges of each pan to loosen BabyCakes. Invert onto saucer, then onto dessert plate, crumb side down.

    Cover and refrigerate BabyCakes for at least 1 hour. Add desired topping just before serving. Serves 4.

SUGGESTED QUICK TOPPING
Glazed green and red grapes.

Maple Walnut BabyCake

Preheat oven to 325°. Place oven rack in center of oven.

Crust

    4 3-inch pans
    1/3 stick margarine
    1/3 cup vanilla cake crumbs
    2/3 cup finely ground English walnuts

Thinly spread bottom and sides of pans with margarine. Evenly coat bottom and sides of pans with nut-crumb mixture and press into place. Save remaining nut-crumb mixture for quick topping. Refrigerate pans while preparing batter.

Batter (Ingredients must be at room temperature.)

    1 8-ounce package cream cheese
    1/4 cup sour cream
    1 egg, beaten
    3/4 cup melted white chocolate
    1/2 teaspoon vanilla
    1/2 cup finely ground English walnuts
    1/4 cup maple syrup

Beat cream cheese until smooth. Add sour cream and egg, mixing thoroughly. Quickly blend in melted chocolate and remaining ingredients. The batter may begin to stiffen as the chocolate cools.

    Pour equal portions of batter into the pans and bake at 325° for 25 to 30 minutes. To check, gently tap pans with flat of fingernail. Cakes are ready when edges are semiset and center still jiggles. Do Not Overbake. Baby-Cakes will continue to bake after they are removed from the oven.

    Remove BabyCakes from the oven and allow to cool about 1 hour, until they reach room temperature.

    Carefully run a smooth knife around the inside edges of each pan to loosen BabyCakes. Invert onto saucer, then onto dessert plate, crumb side down.

    Cover and refrigerate BabyCakes for at least 1 hour. Add desired topping just before serving. Serves 4.

Suggested Quick Topping

Whipped cream sweetened with brown sugar and sprinkled with remaining nut/crumb mixture.

Mocha BabyCake

Preheat oven to 325°. Place oven rack in center of oven.

CRUST

    4 3-inch pans
    1/3 stick margarine
    1 cup chocolate cake crumbs

Thinly spread bottom and sides of pans with margarine. Evenly coat bottom and sides of pans with crumbs and press into place. Save remaining crumbs for next use. Refrigerate pans while preparing batter.

BATTER (Ingredients must be at room temperature.)

    1 8-ounce package cream cheese
    1/4 cup sour cream
    1 egg, beaten
    1 cup melted semisweet chocolate
    1/3 cup strong brewed coffee
    1 tablespoon Tia Maria liqueur

Beat cream cheese until smooth. Add sour cream and egg, mixing thoroughly. Quickly blend in melted chocolate and remaining ingredients. The batter may begin to stiffen as the chocolate cools.

    Pour equal portions of batter into the pans and bake at 325° for 25 to 30 minutes. To check, gently tap pans with flat of fingernail. Cakes are ready when edges are semiset and center still jiggles. DO NOT OVERBAKE. Baby-Cakes will continue to bake after they are removed from the oven.

    Remove BabyCakes from the oven and allow to cool about 1 hour, until they reach room temperature.

    Carefully run a smooth knife around the inside edges of each pan to loosen BabyCakes. Invert onto saucer, then onto dessert plate, crumb side down.

    Cover and refrigerate BabyCakes for at least 1 hour. Add desired topping just before serving. Serves 4.

SUGGESTED QUICK TOPPING

Mocha syrup (1 tablespoon instant coffee dissolved in 1 tablespoon boiling water; add to 1 cup chocolate syrup).

Orange BabyCake

Preheat oven to 325°. Place oven rack in center of oven.

CRUST

    4 3-inch pans
    1/3 stick margarine
    1 cup vanilla cake crumbs

Thinly spread bottom and sides of pans with margarine. Evenly coat bottom and sides of pans with crumbs and press into place. Save remaining crumbs for next use. Refrigerate pans while preparing batter.

BATTER (Ingredients must be at room temperature.)

    1 8-ounce package cream cheese
    1/4 cup sour cream
    1 egg, beaten
    3/4 cup melted white chocolate
    1 tablespoon grated orange peel
    1 teaspoon vanilla
    1/3 cup orange pulp
    1/4 cup curaçao liqueur

Beat cream cheese until smooth. Add sour cream and egg, mixing thoroughly. Quickly blend in melted chocolate and remaining ingredients. The batter may begin to stiffen as the chocolate cools.

Pour equal portions of batter into the pans and bake at 325° for 25 to 30 minutes. To check, gently tap pans with flat of fingernail. Cakes are ready when edges are semiset and center still jiggles. DO NOT OVERBAKE. BabyCakes will continue to bake after they are removed from the oven.

Remove BabyCakes from the oven and allow to cool about 1 hour, until they reach room temperature.

Carefully run a smooth knife around the inside edges of each pan to loosen BabyCakes. Invert onto saucer, then onto dessert plate, crumb side down.

Cover and refrigerate BabyCakes for at least 1 hour. Add desired topping just before serving. Serves 4.

SUGGESTED QUICK TOPPING
Glazed mandarin orange slices drizzled with curaçao.

Orange-Chocolate BabyCake

Preheat oven to 325°. Place oven rack in center of oven.

CRUST

    4 3-inch pans
    1/3 stick margarine
    1 cup chocolate cake crumbs

Thinly spread bottom and sides of pans with margarine. Evenly coat bottom and sides of pans with crumbs and press into place. Save remaining crumbs for next use. Refrigerate pans while preparing batter.

BATTER (Ingredients must be at room temperature.)

    1 8-ounce package cream cheese
    1/4 cup sour cream
    1 egg, beaten
    3/4 cup melted semisweet chocolate
    1/2 cup orange pulp
    1/4 cup curaçao liqueur
    2 tablespoons grated orange peel

Beat cream cheese until smooth. Add sour cream and egg, mixing thoroughly. Quickly blend in melted chocolate and remaining ingredients. The batter may begin to stiffen as the chocolate cools.

Pour equal portions of batter into the pans and bake at 325° for 25 to 30 minutes. To check, gently tap pans with flat of fingernail. Cakes are ready when edges are semiset and center still jiggles. DO NOT OVERBAKE. Baby-Cakes will continue to bake after they are removed from the oven.

Remove BabyCakes from the oven and allow to cool about 1 hour, until they reach room temperature.

Carefully run a smooth knife around the inside edges of each pan to loosen BabyCakes. Invert onto saucer, then onto dessert plate, crumb side down.

Cover and refrigerate BabyCakes for at least 1 hour. Add desired topping just before serving. Serves 4.

SUGGESTED QUICK TOPPING
Whipped cream and mandarin oranges.

Peach BabyCake

Preheat oven to 325°. Place oven rack in center of oven.

Crust

    4 3-inch pans
    1/3 stick margarine
    1 cup vanilla cake crumbs

Thinly spread bottom and sides of pans with margarine. Evenly coat bottom and sides of pans with crumbs and press into place. Save remaining crumbs for next use. Refrigerate pans while preparing batter.

Batter (Ingredients must be at room temperature.)

    1 8-ounce package cream cheese
    1/4 cup sour cream
    1 egg, beaten
    1 cup melted white chocolate
    1/4 cup Southern Comfort whiskey
    1/2 cup pureed peaches

Beat cream cheese until smooth. Add sour cream and egg, mixing thoroughly. Quickly blend in melted chocolate and remaining ingredients. The batter may begin to stiffen as the chocolate cools.

    Pour equal portions of batter into the pans and bake at 325° for 25 to 30 minutes. To check, gently tap pans with flat of fingernail. Cakes are ready when edges are semiset and center still jiggles. DO NOT OVERBAKE. BabyCakes will continue to bake after they are removed from the oven.

    Remove BabyCakes from the oven and allow to cool about 1 hour, until they reach room temperature.

    Carefully run a smooth knife around the inside edges of each pan to loosen BabyCakes. Invert onto saucer, then onto dessert plate, crumb side down.

    Cover and refrigerate BabyCakes for at least 1 hour. Add desired topping just before serving. Serves 4.

Suggested Quick Topping
Fresh sliced peaches and whipped cream.

Piña Colada BabyCake

Preheat oven to 325° Place oven rack in center of oven.

CRUST

 4 3-inch pans
 1/3 stick margarine
 1 cup finely shredded coconut

Thinly spread bottom and sides of pans with margarine. Evenly coat bottom and sides of pans with coconut and press into place. Save remaining coconut for topping. Refrigerate pans while preparing batter.

BATTER (Ingredients must be at room temperature.)

 1 8-ounce package cream cheese
 1 egg, beaten
 1 cup melted white chocolate
 1/3 cup pureed pineapple
 1/3 cup coconut milk
 1 teaspoon rum flavoring

Beat cream cheese until smooth. Add egg, mixing thoroughly. Quickly blend in melted chocolate and remaining ingredients. The batter may begin to stiffen as the chocolate cools.

 Pour equal portions of batter into the pans and bake at 325° for 25 to 30 minutes. To check, gently tap pans with flat of fingernail. Cakes are ready when edges are semiset and center still jiggles. DO NOT OVERBAKE. BabyCakes will continue to bake after they are removed from the oven.

 Remove BabyCakes from the oven and allow to cool about 1 hour, until they reach room temperature.

 Carefully run a smooth knife around the inside edges of each pan to loosen BabyCakes. Invert onto saucer, then onto dessert plate, crumb side down.

 Cover and refrigerate BabyCakes for at least 1 hour. Add desired topping just before serving. Serves 4.

SUGGESTED QUICK TOPPING

Pineapple puree mixed with coconut milk, topped with remaining shredded coconut and a whole maraschino cherry.

Pineapple BabyCake

Preheat oven to 325°. Place oven rack in center of oven.

CRUST

   4 3-inch pans
   1/3 stick margarine
   1 cup lemon cake crumbs

Thinly spread bottom and sides of pans with margarine. Evenly coat bottom and sides of pans with crumbs and press into place. Save remaining crumbs for next use. Refrigerate pans while preparing batter.

BATTER (Ingredients must be at room temperature.)

   1 8-ounce package cream cheese
   1/4 cup sour cream
   1 egg, beaten
   3/4 cup melted white chocolate
   2/3 cup pureed pineapple
   1 tablespoon lemon juice

Beat cream cheese until smooth. Add sour cream and egg, mixing thoroughly. Quickly blend in melted chocolate and remaining ingredients. The batter may begin to stiffen as the chocolate cools.

Pour equal portions of batter into the pans and bake at 325° for 25 to 30 minutes. To check, gently tap pans with flat of fingernail. Cakes are ready when edges are semiset and center still jiggles. DO NOT OVERBAKE. Baby-Cakes will continue to bake after they are removed from the oven.

Remove BabyCakes from the oven and allow to cool about 1 hour, until they reach room temperature.

Carefully run a smooth knife around the inside edges of each pan to loosen BabyCakes. Invert onto saucer, then onto dessert plate, crumb side down.

Cover and refrigerate BabyCakes for at least 1 hour. Add desired topping just before serving. Serves 4.

SUGGESTED QUICK TOPPING
Sliced kiwi fruit and whipped cream.

Pink Peppermint BabyCake

Preheat oven to 325°. Place oven rack in center of oven.

CRUST

    4 3-inch pans
    1/3 stick margarine
    1 cup vanilla cake crumbs

Thinly spread bottom and sides of pans with margarine. Evenly coat bottom and sides of pans with crumbs and press into place. Save remaining crumbs for next use. Refrigerate pans while preparing batter.

BATTER (Ingredients must be at room temperature.)

    1 8-ounce package cream cheese
    1/3 cup sour cream
    1 egg, beaten
    1 cup melted white chocolate
    1/3 cup crushed peppermint sticks
    3 drops red food coloring

Beat cream cheese until smooth. Add sour cream and egg, mixing thoroughly. Quickly blend in melted chocolate and remaining ingredients. The batter may begin to stiffen as the chocolate cools.

    Pour equal portions of batter into the pans and bake at 325° for 25 to 30 minutes. To check, gently tap pans with flat of fingernail. Cakes are ready when edges are semiset and center still jiggles. DO NOT OVERBAKE. Baby-Cakes will continue to bake after they are removed from the oven.

    Remove BabyCakes from the oven and allow to cool about 1 hour, until they reach room temperature.

    Carefully run a smooth knife around the inside edges of each pan to loosen BabyCakes. Invert onto saucer, then onto dessert plate, crumb side down.

    Cover and refrigerate BabyCakes for at least 1 hour. Add desired topping just before serving. Serves 4.

SUGGESTED QUICK TOPPING

Whipped cream sweetened with confectioners' sugar and sprinkled with crushed peppermint candy.

Pomegranate-Tangerine BabyCake

Preheat oven to 325°. Place oven rack in center of oven.

CRUST

    4 3-inch pans
    1/3 stick margarine
    1 cup vanilla cake crumbs

Thinly spread bottom and sides of pans with margarine. Evenly coat bottom and sides of pans with crumbs and press into place. Save remaining crumbs for next use. Refrigerate pans while preparing batter.

BATTER (Ingredients must be at room temperature.)

    1 8-ounce package cream cheese
    1/4 cup sour cream
    1 egg, beaten
    3/4 cup melted white chocolate
    1/3 cup grenadine syrup
    1/3 cup tangerine pulp
    1 tablespoon mandarin Napoleon liqueur

Beat cream cheese until smooth. Add sour cream and egg, mixing thoroughly. Quickly blend in melted chocolate and remaining ingredients. The batter may begin to stiffen as the chocolate cools.

    Pour equal portions of batter into the pans and bake at 325° for 25 to 30 minutes. To check, gently tap pans with flat of fingernail. Cakes are ready when edges are semiset and center still jiggles. DO NOT OVERBAKE. BabyCakes will continue to bake after they are removed from the oven.

    Remove BabyCakes from the oven and allow to cool about 1 hour, until they reach room temperature.

    Carefully run a smooth knife around the inside edges of each pan to loosen BabyCakes. Invert onto saucer, then onto dessert plate, crumb side down.

    Cover and refrigerate BabyCakes for at least 1 hour. Add desired topping just before serving. Serves 4.

SUGGESTED QUICK TOPPING

Sweetened whipped cream drizzled with grenadine syrup and decorated with tangerine peel strips.

Raspberry BabyCake

Preheat oven to 325°. Place oven rack in center of oven.

CRUST

    4 3-inch pans
    1/3 stick margarine
    1 cup vanilla cake crumbs

Thinly spread bottom and sides of pans with margarine. Evenly coat bottom and sides of pans with crumbs and press into place. Save remaining crumbs for next use. Refrigerate pans while preparing batter.

BATTER (Ingredients must be at room temperature.)

    1 8-ounce package cream cheese
    1/4 cup sour cream
    1 egg, beaten
    3/4 cup melted white chocolate
    2 tablespoons framboise liqueur
    2/3 cup crushed raspberries

Beat cream cheese until smooth. Add sour cream and egg, mixing thoroughly. Quickly blend in melted chocolate and remaining ingredients. The batter may begin to stiffen as the chocolate cools.

    Pour equal portions of batter into the pans and bake at 325° for 25 to 30 minutes. To check, gently tap pans with flat of fingernail. Cakes are ready when edges are semiset and center still jiggles. DO NOT OVERBAKE. BabyCakes will continue to bake after they are removed from the oven.

    Remove BabyCakes from the oven and allow to cool about 1 hour, until they reach room temperature.

    Carefully run a smooth knife around the inside edges of each pan to loosen BabyCakes. Invert onto saucer, then onto dessert plate, crumb side down.

    Cover and refrigerate BabyCakes for at least 1 hour. Add desired topping just before serving. Serves 4.

SUGGESTED QUICK TOPPING
Fresh raspberries drizzled with framboise liqueur.

Rocky Road BabyCake

Preheat oven to 325°. Place oven rack in center of oven.

CRUST

    4 3-inch pans
    1/3 stick margarine
    1 cup crushed pecans

Thinly spread bottom and sides of pans with margarine. Evenly coat bottom and sides of pans with nuts and press into place. Save remaining nuts for topping. Refrigerate pans while preparing batter.

BATTER (Ingredients must be at room temperature.)

    1 8-ounce package cream cheese
    1/4 cup sour cream
    1 egg, beaten
    3/4 cup melted semisweet chocolate
    1/2 cup small marshmallows
    1/3 cup crushed pecan pieces

Beat cream cheese until smooth. Add sour cream and egg, mixing thoroughly. Quickly blend in melted chocolate and remaining ingredients. The batter may begin to stiffen as the chocolate cools.

Pour equal portions of batter into the pans and bake at 325° for 25 to 30 minutes. To check, gently tap pans with flat of fingernail. Cakes are ready when edges are semiset and center still jiggles. DO NOT OVERBAKE. Baby-Cakes will continue baking when removed from oven.

Remove BabyCakes from the oven and allow to cool about 1 hour, until they reach room temperature.

Carefully run a smooth knife around the inside edges of each pan to loosen BabyCakes. Invert onto saucer, then onto dessert plate, crumb side down.

Cover and refrigerate BabyCakes for at least 1 hour. Add desired topping just before serving. Serves 4.

SUGGESTED QUICK TOPPING
Chocolate syrup topped with remaining pecan pieces.

Rose Petal BabyCake

Preheat oven to 325°. Place oven rack in center of oven.

Crust

    4 3-inch pans
    1/3 stick margarine
    1 cup vanilla cake crumbs

Thinly spread bottom and sides of pans with margarine. Evenly coat bottom and sides of pans with crumbs and press into place. Save remaining crumbs for next use. Refrigerate pans while preparing batter.

Batter (Ingredients must be at room temperature.)

    1 8-ounce package cream cheese
    1 egg, beaten
    1 cup melted white chocolate
    2 tablespoons sugar
    1/3 cup framboise liqueur
    1/3 cup peach schnapps
    Fresh rose petals

Beat cream cheese until smooth. Add egg, mixing thoroughly. Quickly blend in melted chocolate, sugar, and liqueurs. The batter may begin to stiffen as the chocolate cools.

Pour equal portions of batter into the pans and bake at 325° for 25 to 30 minutes. To check, gently tap pans with flat of fingernail. Cakes are ready when edges are semiset and center still jiggles. DO NOT OVERBAKE. Baby-Cakes will continue to bake after they are removed from the oven.

Remove BabyCakes from the oven and allow to cool about 1 hour, until they reach room temperature.

Carefully run a smooth knife around the inside edges of each pan to loosen BabyCakes. Invert onto saucer, then onto dessert plate, crumb side down.

Cover and refrigerate BabyCakes for at least 1 hour. Add desired topping just before serving. Serves 4.

Suggested Quick Topping

Brush rose petals with egg white and sprinkle with granulated sugar. Decorate cakes with whipped cream and rose petals (which can be eaten).

Tia Hanna's BabyCake

(Uses no white chocolate)
Preheat oven to 325°. Place oven rack in center of oven.

Crust

    4 3-inch pans
    1/3 stick margarine
    1 cup graham cracker crumbs

Thinly spread bottom and sides of pans with margarine. Evenly coat bottom and sides of pans with crumbs and press into place. Bake at 325° for 15 minutes. Set aside to cool. Save remaining crumbs for next use.

Batter (Ingredients must be at room temperature.)

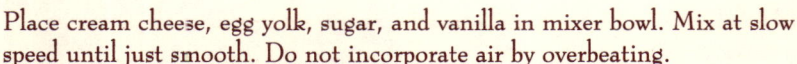

    1 8-ounce package cream cheese
    1 egg yolk
    1/2 cup sugar
    1 teaspoon vanilla
    1/2 cup milk
    1 1/2 tablespoons flour
    1 egg white

Place cream cheese, egg yolk, sugar, and vanilla in mixer bowl. Mix at slow speed until just smooth. Do not incorporate air by overbeating.

Slowly add milk and flour, alternating additions. Set batter aside.

Beat egg white until stiff. Fold gently into batter.

Pour equal portions of batter into the pans and bake 25 to 30 minutes at 325°. To check, gently tap pans with flat of fingernail. Cakes are ready when edges are semiset and center still jiggles. DO NOT OVERBAKE. BabyCakes will continue to bake after they are removed from the oven.

Remove BabyCakes from the oven and allow to cool about 1 hour, until they reach room temperature.

When pans are cool, carefully run a smooth knife around the inside edges of each pan to loosen BabyCakes. Invert onto saucer, then onto dessert plate, crumb side down.

Cover and refrigerate BabyCakes for at least 1 hour. Add desired topping just before serving. Serves 4.

Suggested Quick Topping
Plain or sprinkled with confectioners' sugar.

Tiger Stripe BabyCake

Preheat oven to 325°. Place oven rack in center of oven.

CRUST

    4 3-inch pans
    1/3 stick margarine
    1 cup chocolate cake crumbs

Thinly spread bottom and sides of pans with margarine. Evenly coat bottom and sides of pans with crumbs and press into place. Save remaining crumbs for next use. Refrigerate pans while preparing batter.

BATTER (Ingredients must be at room temperature.)

    1 8-ounce package cream cheese
    1/4 cup sour cream
    1 egg, beaten
    1/3 cup smooth peanut butter
    1/4 cup melted white chocolate
    3/4 cup melted semisweet chocolate

Beat cream cheese until smooth. Add sour cream and egg, mixing thoroughly.

Divide this mixture evenly between two bowls. Combine the peanut butter and melted white chocolate and thoroughly mix into one-half of the cream cheese mixture; mix the semisweet chocolate into the other half.

Then gently swirl the peanut butter mixture into the chocolate mixture. (Only swirl it; do not combine the two flavors into one.)

Divide the swirled batter equally among the pans and bake at 325° for 25 to 30 minutes. To check, gently tap pans with flat of fingernail. Cakes are ready when edges are semiset and center still jiggles. DO NOT OVERBAKE. BabyCakes will continue to bake after they are removed from the oven.

Remove BabyCakes from the oven and allow to cool about 1 hour, until they reach room temperature.

Carefully run a smooth knife around the inside edges of each pan to loosen BabyCakes. Invert onto saucer, then onto dessert plate, crumb side down.

Cover and refrigerate BabyCakes for at least 1 hour. Add desired topping just before serving. Serves 4.

SUGGESTED QUICK TOPPING
Whipped cream and chocolate sprinkles.

Tofu BabyCake

Preheat oven to 325°. Place oven rack in center of oven.

CRUST

    4 3-inch pans
    1/3 stick margarine
    1 cup vanilla cake crumbs

Thinly spread bottom and sides of pans with margarine. Evenly coat bottom and sides of pans with crumbs and press into place. Save remaining crumbs for next use. Refrigerate pans while preparing batter.

BATTER (Ingredients must be at room temperature.)

    12 ounces medium-consistency tofu
    1/4 cup pureed cottage cheese
    3/4 cup sugar
    1 teaspoon vanilla or other flavoring
    1 tablespoon lemon juice
    1/2 teaspoon grated lemon peel
    3 egg whites

Place tofu in mixer bowl. Mix at high speed until smooth. Continue mixing while adding pureed cottage cheese, sugar, vanilla, lemon juice, grated lemon peel, and egg whites.

Divide the batter among the pans. Put batter-filled pans 2 inches apart into oven and bake 25 to 30 minutes at 325°.

To check, gently tap batter pans with flat of fingernail. Cakes are ready when edges are semiset and center still jiggles. DO NOT OVERBAKE. BabyCakes will continue to bake after they are removed from the oven.

Carefully remove BabyCakes from the oven. Allow to cool about 1 hour, until they reach room temperature.

When pans are cool, carefully run a smooth knife around the inside edges of each pan to loosen BabyCakes. Invert onto saucer, then onto dessert plate, crumb side down.

Cover and refrigerate BabyCakes for at least 1 hour. Add desired topping just before serving. Serves 4.

SUGGESTED QUICK TOPPING
Glazed bananas and fresh strawberries.

Refrigerator BabyCakes

If you want to cut down on cholesterol and calories and save preparation time, try Refrigerator BabyCakes. The recipes in this section call for gelatin instead of eggs, and chocolate as the setting agent. Allow about one and a half hours for preparation time.

The texture of Refrigerator BabyCakes is lighter, and their flavors are livelier than the baked BabyCakes—very refreshing on hot summer days or after rich meals.

Add extra crumbs to the bottom of the pans so the Refrigerator BabyCakes will detach easily when inverted.

Feel free to experiment and have fun!

Almond-Chocolate Refrigerator BabyCake

CRUST

    4 3-inch pans
    1/3 stick margarine
    1 cup chocolate wafer crumbs

Thinly spread bottom and sides of pans with margarine. Evenly coat bottom and sides of pans with crumbs and press into place. Add additional crumbs to the bottom of each pan so the cakes can be easily removed when chilled. Save remaining crumbs for next use. Refrigerate pans while preparing batter.

BATTER

    1 envelope unflavored gelatin
    1/4 cup warm water
    1 8-ounce package cream cheese
    1/2 cup sour cream
    1 4-ounce package regular chocolate pudding (cooked with only 1 cup milk)
    1 teaspoon almond flavoring

Soften gelatin in warm water for 5 minutes. Stir until dissolved. Mix gelatin, cream cheese, and sour cream together. Add remaining ingredients to cream cheese mixture, continuing to mix until well blended.

Pour equal portions of batter into pans and chill until firm.

Carefully run a smooth knife around the inside edges of each pan to loosen Refrigerator BabyCakes. Invert onto saucer, then onto dessert plate, crumb side down.

Add desired topping. Serves 4.

SUGGESTED QUICK TOPPING
Chocolate syrup and crushed almonds.

Amaretto Refrigerator BabyCake

CRUST

    4 3-inch pans
    1/3 stick margarine
    1 cup vanilla wafer crumbs

Thinly spread bottom and sides of pans with margarine. Evenly coat bottom and sides of pans with crumbs and press into place. Add additional crumbs to the bottom of each pan so the cakes can be easily removed when chilled. Save remaining crumbs for next use. Refrigerate pans while preparing batter.

BATTER

    1 envelope unflavored gelatin
    1/4 cup warm water
    1 8-ounce package cream cheese
    1/2 cup sour cream
    1/4 cup amaretto liqueur
    1 teaspoon almond flavoring
    1 4-ounce package regular vanilla
        pudding (cooked with only 1 cup milk)

Soften gelatin in warm water for 5 minutes. Stir until dissolved. Mix gelatin, cream cheese, and sour cream together. Add amaretto and almond flavoring to pudding mix. Then add pudding mixture to cream cheese mixture, continuing to mix until well blended.

    Pour equal portions of batter into pans and chill until firm.

    Carefully run a smooth knife around the inside edges of each pan to loosen Refrigerator BabyCakes. Invert onto saucer, then onto dessert plate, crumb side down.

    Add desired topping. Serves 4.

SUGGESTED QUICK TOPPING
Chocolate syrup.

Apricot Refrigerator BabyCake

CRUST

    4 3-inch pans
    1/3 stick margarine
    1 cup vanilla wafer crumbs

Thinly spread bottom and sides of pans with margarine. Evenly coat bottom and sides of pans with crumbs and press into place. Add additional crumbs to the bottom of each pan so the cakes can be easily removed when chilled. Save remaining crumbs for next use. Refrigerate pans while preparing batter.

BATTER

    1 envelope unflavored gelatin
    1/4 cup warm water
    1 8-ounce package cream cheese
    1/2 cup sugar
    1/2 cup sour cream
    1/4 cup apricot nectar
    1/2 cup chopped canned apricots

Soften gelatin in warm water for 5 minutes. Stir until dissolved. Mix gelatin, cream cheese, sugar, sour cream, and apricot nectar together. Add chopped apricots to cream cheese mixture, continuing to mix until well blended.

    Pour equal portions into pans and chill until firm.

    Carefully run a smooth knife around the inside edges of each pan to loosen Refrigerator BabyCakes. Invert onto saucer, then onto dessert plate, crumb side down.

    Add desired topping. Serves 4.

SUGGESTED QUICK TOPPING
Apricot slices soaked in curaçao.

Black Bottom Refrigerator BabyCake

CRUST

    4 3-inch pans
    1/3 stick margarine
    1 cup chocolate wafer crumbs

Thinly spread bottom and sides of pans with margarine. Evenly coat bottom and sides of pans with crumbs and press into place. Add additional crumbs to the bottom of each pan so the cakes can be easily removed when chilled. Save remaining crumbs for next use. Refrigerate pans while preparing batter.

BATTER

    1 envelope unflavored gelatin
    1/4 cup warm water
    1 8-ounce package cream cheese
    1/2 cup sugar
    2/3 cup cooked chocolate pudding
    3 tablespoons brandy
    2/3 cup cooked vanilla pudding

Soften gelatin in warm water for 5 minutes. Stir until dissolved. Mix cream cheese and sugar together. Add gelatin to cream cheese mixture, continuing to mix until well blended. Divide this mixture in half, using two small bowls. Add chocolate pudding to one half; add brandy and vanilla pudding to the other half.

    Make the black-bottom layer by putting the chocolate mixture into each pan first. Top this chocolate layer with the vanilla-brandy mixture. Chill until firm.

    Carefully run a smooth knife around the inside edges of each pan to loosen Refrigerator BabyCakes. Invert onto saucer, then onto dessert plate, crumb side down.

    Add desired topping. Serves 4.

SUGGESTED QUICK TOPPING
Drizzle with chocolate syrup.

Black Forest Refrigerator BabyCake

CRUST

    4 3-inch pans
    $1/3$ stick margarine
    1 cup chocolate wafer crumbs

Thinly spread bottom and sides of pans with margarine. Evenly coat bottom and sides of pans with crumbs and press into place. Add additional crumbs to the bottom of each pan so the cakes can be easily removed when chilled. Save remaining crumbs for next use. Refrigerate pans while preparing batter.

BATTER

    1 envelope unflavored gelatin
    $1/4$ cup warm water
    1 8-ounce package cream cheese
    $1/4$ cup sour cream
    1 4-ounce package regular chocolate pudding (cooked with only 1 cup milk)

Soften gelatin in warm water for 5 minutes. Stir until dissolved. Mix gelatin, cream cheese, and sour cream until well blended. Add pudding to cream cheese mixture, continuing to mix until well blended.

    Pour equal portions of batter into pans and chill until firm.

    Carefully run a smooth knife around the inside edges of each pan to loosen Refrigerator BabyCakes. Invert onto saucer, then onto dessert plate, crumb side down.

    Add desired topping. Serves 4.

SUGGESTED QUICK TOPPING
Cherry pie filling and whipped topping.

Blueberry Refrigerator BabyCake

CRUST

    4 3-inch pans
    $1/3$ stick margarine
    1 cup vanilla wafer crumbs

Thinly spread bottom and sides of pans with margarine. Evenly coat bottom and sides of pans with crumbs and press into place. Add additional crumbs to the bottom of each pan so the cakes can be easily removed when chilled. Save remaining crumbs for next use. Refrigerate pans while preparing batter.

BATTER

    1 envelope unflavored gelatin
    $1/4$ cup warm water
    1 8-ounce package cream cheese
    $1/2$ cup sugar
    $1/2$ cup sour cream
    1 tablespoon lemon juice
    $3/4$ cup blueberry pie filling

Soften gelatin in warm water for 5 minutes. Stir until dissolved. Mix gelatin, cream cheese, sugar, and sour cream. Add remaining ingredients to cream cheese mixture, continuing to mix until well blended.

    Pour equal portions of batter into pans and chill until firm.

    Carefully run a smooth knife around the inside edges of each pan to loosen Refrigerator BabyCakes. Invert onto saucer, then onto dessert plate, crumb side down.

    Add desired topping. Serves 4.

SUGGESTED QUICK TOPPING
Glazed blueberries or blueberry pie filling.

Brandy Alexander Refrigerator BabyCake

Crust

    4 3-inch pans
    1/3 stick margarine
    1 cup chocolate wafer crumbs

Thinly spread bottom and sides of pans with margarine. Evenly coat bottom and sides of pans with crumbs and press into place. Add additional crumbs to the bottom of each pan so the cakes can be easily removed when chilled. Save remaining crumbs for next use. Refrigerate pans while preparing batter.

Batter

    1 envelope unflavored gelatin
    1/4 cup warm water
    1 8-ounce package cream cheese
    1/4 cup sour cream
    1/4 cup sugar
    1/4 cup brandy
    1 teaspoon nutmeg
    3/4 cup chocolate syrup

Soften gelatin in warm water for 5 minutes. Stir until dissolved. Mix gelatin, cream cheese, and sour cream together. Add remaining ingredients to cream cheese mixture, continuing to mix until well blended.

    Pour equal portions of batter into pans and chill until firm.

    Carefully run a smooth knife around the inside edges of each pan to loosen Refrigerator BabyCakes. Invert onto saucer, then onto dessert plate, crumb side down.

    Add desired topping. Serves 4.

Suggested Quick Topping
Sweetened whipped cream, sprinkled with cocoa and nutmeg.

Cherry Refrigerator BabyCake

CRUST

    4 3-inch pans
    1/3 stick margarine
    1 cup vanilla wafer crumbs

Thinly spread bottom and sides of pans with margarine. Evenly coat bottom and sides of pans with crumbs and press into place. Add additional crumbs to the bottom of each pan so the cakes can be easily removed when chilled. Save remaining crumbs for next use. Refrigerate pans while preparing batter.

BATTER

    1 envelope unflavored gelatin
    1/4 cup warm water
    1 8-ounce package cream cheese
    1/2 cup sugar
    1/2 cup sour cream
    3/4 cup maraschino cherry bits

Soften gelatin in warm water for 5 minutes. Stir until dissolved. Mix gelatin, cream cheese, sugar, and sour cream together. Add maraschino cherry bits to cream cheese mixture, continuing to mix until well blended.

    Pour equal portions of batter into pans and chill until firm.

    Carefully run a smooth knife around the inside edges of each pan to loosen Refrigerator BabyCakes. Invert onto saucer, then onto dessert plate, crumb side down.

    Add desired topping. Serves 4.

SUGGESTED QUICK TOPPING
Whole maraschino cherries.

Chocolate Refrigerator BabyCake

CRUST

    4 3-inch pans
    1/3 stick margarine
    1 cup chocolate wafer crumbs

Thinly spread bottom and sides of pans with margarine. Evenly coat bottom and sides of pans with crumbs and press into place. Add additional crumbs to the bottom of each pan so the cakes can be easily removed when chilled. Save remaining crumbs for next use. Refrigerate pans while preparing batter.

BATTER

    1 envelope unflavored gelatin
    1/4 cup warm water
    1 8-ounce package cream cheese
    1/4 cup sour cream
    1/4 cup sugar
    1 cup chocolate syrup
    1/4 cup cocoa

Soften gelatin in warm water for 5 minutes. Stir until dissolved. Mix gelatin, cream cheese, and sour cream together. Add remaining ingredients to cream cheese mixture, continuing to mix until well blended.

Pour equal portions of batter into pans and chill until firm.

Carefully run a smooth knife around the inside edges of each pan to loosen Refrigerator BabyCakes. Invert onto saucer, then onto dessert plate, crumb side down.

Add desired topping. Serves 4.

SUGGESTED QUICK TOPPING
Plain or glazed fresh strawberries.

Chocolate-Hazelnut Refrigerator BabyCake

CRUST

    4 3-inch pans
    1/3 stick margarine
    1 cup crushed hazelnuts

Thinly spread bottom and sides of pans with margarine. Evenly coat bottom and sides of pans with nuts and press into place. Add additional nuts to the bottom of each pan so the cakes can be easily removed when chilled. Save remaining nuts for topping. Refrigerate pans while preparing batter.

BATTER

    1 envelope unflavored gelatin
    1/4 cup warm water
    1 8-ounce package cream cheese
    1/2 cup sour cream
    1/4 cup crushed hazelnuts
    1 teaspoon butternut flavoring
    1 cup chocolate syrup

Soften gelatin in warm water for 5 minutes. Stir until dissolved. Mix gelatin, cream cheese, and sour cream together. Add remaining ingredients to cream cheese mixture, continuing to mix until well blended.

    Pour equal portions of batter into pans and chill until firm.

    Carefully run a smooth knife around the inside edges of each pan to loosen Refrigerator BabyCakes. Invert onto saucer, then onto dessert plate, crumb side down.

    Add desired topping. Serves 4.

SUGGESTED QUICK TOPPING
Chocolate syrup and crushed hazelnuts.

Cosmopolitan Refrigerator BabyCake

CRUST

    4 3-inch pans
    1/3 stick margarine
    1 cup vanilla wafer crumbs

Thinly spread bottom and sides of pans with margarine. Evenly coat bottom and sides of pans with crumbs and press into place. Add additional crumbs to the bottom of each pan so the cakes can be easily removed when chilled. Save remaining crumbs for next use. Refrigerate pans while preparing batter.

BATTER

    1 envelope unflavored gelatin
    1/4 cup warm water
    1 8-ounce package cream cheese
    3/4 cup sugar
    1/2 cup sour cream
    1/4 cup orange juice
    2 tablespoons lemon juice

Soften gelatin in warm water for 5 minutes. Stir until dissolved. Mix gelatin, cream cheese, sugar, and sour cream together. Add remaining ingredients to cream cheese mixture, continuing to mix until well blended.

Pour equal portions of batter into pans and chill until firm.

Carefully run a smooth knife around the inside edges of each pan to loosen Refrigerator BabyCakes. Invert onto saucer, then onto dessert plate, crumb side down.

Add desired topping. Serves 4.

SUGGESTED QUICK TOPPING
Glazed fresh strawberries.

Eggnog Refrigerator BabyCake

CRUST

    4 3-inch pans
    1/3 stick margarine
    1 cup finely ground pecans

Thinly spread bottom and sides of pans with margarine. Evenly coat bottom and sides of pans with nuts and press into place. Add additional nuts to the bottom of each pan so the cakes can be easily removed when chilled. Save remaining nuts for topping. Refrigerate pans while preparing batter.

BATTER

    1 envelope unflavored gelatin
    1/4 cup warm water
    1 8-ounce package cream cheese
    1/4 cup sugar
    1 cup prepared eggnog
    1 teaspoon nutmeg
    1/4 cup brandy

Soften gelatin in warm water for 5 minutes. Stir until dissolved. Mix gelatin, cream cheese, sugar, and eggnog together. Add remaining ingredients to cream cheese mixture, continuing to mix until well blended.

Pour equal portions of batter into pans and chill until firm.

Carefully run a smooth knife around the inside edges of each pan to loosen Refrigerator BabyCakes. Invert onto saucer, then onto dessert plate, crumb side down.

Add desired topping. Serves 4.

SUGGESTED QUICK TOPPING
Sweetened whipped cream sprinkled with remaining ground pecans.

Ginger-Chocolate Refrigerator BabyCake

CRUST

    4 3-inch pans
    1/3 stick margarine
    1 cup gingersnap crumbs

Thinly spread bottom and sides of pans with margarine. Evenly coat bottom and sides of pans with crumbs and press into place. Add additional crumbs to the bottom of each pan so the cakes can be easily removed when chilled. Save remaining crumbs for next use. Refrigerate pans while preparing batter.

BATTER

    1 envelope unflavored gelatin
    1/4 cup warm water
    1 8-ounce package cream cheese
    1/4 cup sugar
    3/4 cup sour cream
    1/2 teaspoon powered ginger
    3/4 cup chocolate syrup

Soften gelatin in warm water for 5 minutes. Stir until dissolved. Mix gelatin, cream cheese, sugar, and sour cream together. Add remaining ingredients to cream cheese mixture, continuing to mix until well blended.

    Pour equal portions of batter into the pans and chill until firm.

    Carefully run a smooth knife around the inside edges of each pan to loosen Refrigerator BabyCakes. Invert onto saucer, then onto dessert plate, crumb side down.

    Add desired topping. Serves 4.

SUGGESTED QUICK TOPPING
Whipped topping dusted with cocoa.

Irish Cream Refrigerator BabyCake

Crust

    4 3-inch pans
    1/3 stick margarine
    1 cup chocolate wafer crumbs

Thinly spread bottom and sides of pans with margarine. Evenly coat bottom and sides of pans with crumbs and press into place. Add additional crumbs to the bottom of each pan so the cakes can be easily removed when chilled. Save remaining crumbs for next use. Refrigerate pans while preparing batter.

Batter

    1 envelope unflavored gelatin
    1/4 cup warm water
    1 8-ounce package cream cheese
    1/4 cup sugar
    1/4 cup sour cream
    1/4 cup Irish cream liqueur
    3/4 cup chocolate syrup

Soften gelatin in warm water for 5 minutes. Stir until dissolved. Mix gelatin, cream cheese, sugar, and sour cream together. Add remaining ingredients to cream cheese mixture, continuing to mix until well blended.

Pour equal portions of batter into the pans and chill until firm.

Carefully run a smooth knife around the inside edges of each pan to loosen Refrigerator BabyCakes. Invert onto saucer, then onto dessert plate, crumb side down.

Add desired topping. Serves 4.

Suggested Quick Topping
Chocolate syrup mixed with Irish cream liqueur.

Lemon Refrigerator BabyCake

CRUST

    4 3-inch pans
    1/3 stick margarine
    1 cup chocolate wafer crumbs

Thinly spread bottom and sides of pans with margarine. Evenly coat bottom and sides of pans with crumbs and press into place. Add additional crumbs to the bottom of each pan so the cakes can be easily removed when chilled. Save remaining crumbs for topping. Refrigerate pans while preparing batter.

BATTER

    1 envelope unflavored gelatin
    1/4 cup warm water
    1 8-ounce package cream cheese
    3/4 cup sugar
    1/2 cup sour cream
    1/2 cup lemon juice
    1 tablespoon grated lemon rind

Soften gelatin in warm water for 5 minutes. Stir until dissolved. Mix gelatin, cream cheese, sugar, and sour cream together. Add remaining ingredients to cream cheese mixture, continuing to mix until well blended.

    Pour equal portions of batter into the pans and chill until firm.

    Carefully run a smooth knife around the inside edges of each pan to loosen Refrigerator BabyCakes. Invert onto saucer, then onto dessert plate, crumb side down.

    Add desired topping. Serves 4.

SUGGESTED QUICK TOPPING
Crushed chocolate wafer crumbs.

Lime Refrigerator BabyCake

CRUST

    4 3-inch pans
    1/3 stick margarine
    1 cup vanilla wafer crumbs

Thinly spread bottom and sides of pans with margarine. Evenly coat bottom and sides of pans with crumbs and press into place. Add additional crumbs to the bottom of each pan so the cakes can be easily removed when chilled. Save remaining crumbs for next use. Refrigerate pans while preparing batter.

BATTER

    1 envelope unflavored gelatin
    1/4 cup warm water
    1 8-ounce package cream cheese
    3/4 cup sugar
    1/2 cup sour cream
    1/2 cup lime juice
    1 tablespoon grated lime rind

Soften gelatin in warm water for 5 minutes. Stir until dissolved. Mix gelatin, cream cheese, sugar, and sour cream together. Add remaining ingredients to cream cheese mixture, continuing to mix until well blended.

    Pour equal portions of batter into the pans and chill until firm.

    Carefully run a smooth knife around the inside edges of each pan to loosen Refrigerator BabyCakes. Invert onto saucer, then onto dessert plate, crumb side down.

    Add desired topping. Serves 4.

SUGGESTED QUICK TOPPING
Whipped topping and curled lime slices.

Marble Refrigerator BabyCake

CRUST

- 4 3-inch pans
- 1/3 stick margarine
- 1 cup chocolate wafer crumbs

Thinly spread bottom and sides of pans with margarine. Evenly coat bottom and sides of pans with crumbs and press into place. Add additional crumbs to the bottom of each pan so the cakes can be easily removed when chilled. Save remaining crumbs for next use. Refrigerate pans while preparing batter.

BATTER

- 1 envelope unflavored gelatin
- 1/4 cup warm water
- 1 8-ounce package cream cheese
- 1/4 cup sugar
- 1/2 cup sour cream
- 1/2 cup melted semisweet chocolate
- 1/2 cup melted white chocolate

Soften gelatin in warm water for 5 minutes. Stir until dissolved. Mix gelatin, cream cheese, sour cream, and sugar until well blended.

Pour equal portions of batter into two bowls. Thoroughly mix the melted semisweet chocolate into one-half of the cream cheese mixture; mix the melted white chocolate into the other half.

Gently swirl the semisweet chocolate mixture into the white chocolate mixture. (Do not combine the two mixtures into one.) Carefully pour the swirled mixture into the pans and chill until firm.

Run a smooth knife around the inside edges of each pan to loosen Refrigerator BabyCakes. Invert onto saucer, then onto dessert plate, crumb side down.

Add desired topping. Serves 4.

SUGGESTED QUICK TOPPING
Whipped topping drizzled with chocolate syrup.

Mocha Refrigerator BabyCake

CRUST

- 4 3-inch pans
- 1/3 stick margarine
- 1 cup vanilla wafer crumbs

Thinly spread bottom and sides of pans with margarine. Evenly coat bottom and sides of pans with crumbs and press into place. Add additional crumbs to the bottom of each pan so the cakes can be easily removed when chilled. Save remaining crumbs for next use. Refrigerate pans while preparing batter.

BATTER

- 1 envelope unflavored gelatin
- 1/4 cup warm water
- 1 8-ounce package cream cheese
- 1/4 cup sour cream
- 1/4 cup sugar
- 3/4 cup chocolate syrup
- 2 tablespoons Tia Maria liqueur
- 1/4 cup strong brewed coffee

Soften gelatin in warm water for 5 minutes. Stir until dissolved. Mix gelatin, cream cheese, sour cream, and sugar together. Add remaining ingredients to cream cheese mixture, continuing to mix until well blended.

Pour equal portions of batter into the pans and chill until firm.

Carefully run a smooth knife around the inside edges of each pan to loosen Refrigerator BabyCakes. Invert onto saucer, then onto dessert plate, crumb side down.

Add desired topping. Serves 4.

SUGGESTED QUICK TOPPING
Whipped topping drizzled with chocolate syrup.

Orange Refrigerator BabyCake

CRUST

    4 3-inch pans
    1/3 stick margarine
    1 cup vanilla wafer crumbs

Thinly spread bottom and sides of pans with margarine. Evenly coat bottom and sides of pans with crumbs and press into place. Add additional crumbs to the bottom of each pan so the cakes can be easily removed when chilled. Save remaining crumbs for next use. Refrigerate pans while preparing batter.

BATTER

    1 envelope unflavored gelatin
    1/4 cup warm water
    1 8-ounce package cream cheese
    1/2 cup sugar
    1/4 cup sour cream
    1 cup orange pulp and juice
    2 tablespoons grated orange peel

Soften gelatin in warm water for 5 minutes. Stir until dissolved. Mix gelatin, cream cheese, sugar, and sour cream together. Add remaining ingredients to cream cheese mixture, continuing to mix until well blended.

Pour equal portions of batter into pans and chill until firm.

Carefully run a smooth knife around the inside edges of each pan to loosen Refrigerator BabyCakes. Invert onto saucer, then onto dessert plate, crumb side down.

Add desired topping. Serves 4.

SUGGESTED QUICK TOPPING
Whipped topping and mandarin orange slices.

Peach Refrigerator BabyCake

Crust

    4 3-inch pans
    1/3 stick margarine
    1 cup vanilla wafer crumbs

Thinly spread bottom and sides of pans with margarine. Evenly coat bottom and sides of pans with crumbs and press into place. Add additional crumbs to the bottom of each pan so the cakes can be easily removed when chilled. Save remaining crumbs for next use. Refrigerate pans while preparing batter.

Batter

    1 envelope unflavored gelatin
    1/4 cup warm water
    1 8-ounce package cream cheese
    1/2 cup sugar
    1/4 cup sour cream
    1/2 cup pureed peaches
    1/4 cup peach schnapps

Soften gelatin in warm water for 5 minutes. Stir until dissolved. Mix gelatin, cream cheese, sugar, and sour cream together. Add remaining ingredients to cream cheese mixture, continuing to mix until well blended.

Pour equal portions of batter into the pans and chill until firm.

Carefully run a smooth knife around the inside edges of each pan to loosen Refrigerator BabyCakes. Invert onto saucer, then onto dessert plate, crumb side down.

Add desired topping. Serves 4.

Suggested Quick Topping
Glazed fresh peaches.

Pineapple Refrigerator BabyCake

Crust

    4 3-inch pans
    1/3 stick margarine
    1 cup vanilla wafer crumbs

Thinly spread bottom and sides of pans with margarine. Evenly coat bottom and sides of pans with crumbs and press into place. Add additional crumbs to the bottom of each pan so the cakes can be easily removed when chilled. Save remaining crumbs for next use. Refrigerate pans while preparing batter.

Batter

    1 envelope unflavored gelatin
    1/4 cup warm water
    1 8-ounce package cream cheese
    1/2 cup sugar
    1/4 cup sour cream
    1 cup pureed pineapple (canned)
    2 tablespoons lemon juice

Soften gelatin in warm water for 5 minutes. Stir until dissolved. Mix gelatin, cream cheese, sugar, and sour cream together. Add remaining ingredients to cream cheese mixture, continuing to mix until well blended.

    Pour equal portions of batter into the pans and chill until firm.

    Carefully run a smooth knife around the inside edges of each pan to loosen Refrigerator BabyCakes. Invert onto saucer, then onto dessert plate, crumb side down.

    Add desired topping. Serves 4.

Suggested Quick Topping
Sweetened sour cream combined with crushed pineapple.

Strawberry Refrigerator BabyCake

CRUST

    4 3-inch pans
    $1/3$ stick margarine
    1 cup vanilla wafer crumbs

Thinly spread bottom and sides of pans with margarine. Evenly coat bottom and sides of pans with crumbs and press into place. Add additional crumbs to the bottom of each pan so the cakes can be easily removed when chilled. Save remaining crumbs for next use. Refrigerate pans while preparing batter.

BATTER

    1 envelope unflavored gelatin
    $1/4$ cup warm water
    1 8-ounce package cream cheese
    $1/4$ cup sugar
    $1/2$ cup sour cream
    1 cup pureed sweetened strawberries
    2 tablespoons lemon juice

Soften gelatin in warm water for 5 minutes. Stir until dissolved. Mix gelatin, cream cheese, sugar, and sour cream together. Add remaining ingredients to cream cheese mixture, continuing to mix until well blended.

    Pour equal portions of batter into the pans and chill until firm.

    Carefully run a smooth knife around the inside edges of each pan to loosen Refrigerator BabyCakes. Invert onto saucer, then onto dessert plate, crumb side down.

    Add desired topping. Serves 4.

SUGGESTED QUICK TOPPING
Glazed fresh strawberries.

Turtle Walk Refrigerator BabyCake

CRUST

    4 3-inch pans
    1/3 stick margarine
    1 cup vanilla wafer crumbs

Thinly spread bottom and sides of pans with margarine. Evenly coat bottom and sides of pans with crumbs and press into place. Add additional crumbs to the bottom of each pan so the cakes can be easily removed when chilled. Save remaining crumbs for next use. Refrigerate pans while preparing batter.

BATTER

    1/4 cup soft caramel candies
    1/2 cup semisweet chocolate bits
    1/4 cup finely ground pecans
    1 envelope unflavored gelatin
    1/4 cup warm water
    1 8-ounce package cream cheese
    1/4 cup sour cream
    1/2 cup sugar
    1/4 cup cocoa powder

Stir caramel candies and chocolate bits over low heat until melted. Add pecans. Keep warm. Soften gelatin in warm water for 5 minutes. Stir until dissolved. Mix gelatin, cream cheese, sour cream, and sugar until well blended. Mix in cocoa powder. Mix 1/2 cup of cream cheese mixture into chocolate-caramel mixture, and spoon into pans to make bottom layer. Spoon remaining cream cheese mixture on top of the chocolate-caramel mixture in the pans. Chill until firm.

    Carefully run a smooth knife around the inside edges of each pan to loosen Refrigerator BabyCakes. Invert onto saucer, then onto dessert plate, crumb side down.

    Add desired topping. Serves 4.

SUGGESTED QUICK TOPPING
Chocolate syrup and chocolate curls.

Toppings

BabyCakes are delights in themselves. Adding toppings from this section makes them truly elegant cheesecakes that please the eye as well as the palate.

Choose from glazed fresh fruits, a baked meringue, flavorful fruit sauces, and even a rich nut topping to create desserts your guests will remember for a long time to come.

Toppings

BLUEBERRY–LEMON PEEL TOPPING

    1/2 cup water
    1/4 cup sugar
    1 tablespoon lemon juice
    Peel of 1 lemon in julienne strips
    1 cup blueberry pie filling

Mix water, sugar, and lemon juice. Bring to a boil, stirring occasionally.

Add lemon peel strips and boil for 2 minutes. Remove from heat and allow peel to steep in liquid for 1 hour. Remove lemon peel and mix 1 tablespoon lemon liquid into blueberry pie filling, discarding remaining lemon liquid.

Top BabyCakes with blueberry pie filling and decorate with lemon peel.

BRANDIED APRICOT TOPPING

    1/4 cup brandy
    1 teaspoon lemon juice
    1/4 cup canned apricot nectar
    1/3 cup sugar
    1/2 pound dried apricots
    1 tablespoon cornstarch

Combine brandy, lemon juice, apricot nectar, and sugar in a saucepan. Heat and stir to dissolve sugar. Remove from heat and add dried apricots. Let stand for 24 hours, turning apricots occasionally.

Remove plumped apricots and add cornstarch to liquids. Bring to a boil to thicken. Remove from heat and add apricots. Cool to room temperature.

Brush the top of BabyCake with sauce, arrange apricots on top, and drizzle sauce over apricots.

Toppings

BUTTERSCOTCH TOPPING

    1/4 cup packed brown sugar
    3 tablespoons light corn syrup
    2 tablespoons margarine
    1 teaspoon vanilla
    1/2 cup butterscotch bits

Combine brown sugar, corn syrup, and margarine in small saucepan. Bring to boil, stirring. Remove from heat and add vanilla and butterscotch bits. Stir to melt butterscotch bits and drizzle over BabyCakes.

GLAZED FRESH FRUIT (Quick and Easy)

    2 cups any fresh fruit
    3/4 cup light corn syrup

Simmer syrup 5 minutes and allow to cool for 1 hour. Gently toss fruit in warm corn syrup, making certain syrup covers each piece of fruit.

    Place glazed fruits in a colander to drain for 5 minutes. Decorate BabyCakes.

GRASSHOPPER TOPPING

    1/4 cup chocolate syrup
    1/4 cup creme de menthe

Mix chocolate syrup with creme de menthe and simmer for 5 minutes. Add confectioners' sugar if a thicker topping is desired. Drizzle warm topping over BabyCakes.

Toppings

Hazelnut Topping

   $1/4$ cup finely ground hazelnuts (filberts)
   $1/2$ cup Frangelica liqueur
   1 tablespoon cornstarch

Combine hazelnuts and Frangelica. Mix cornstarch with 1/2 cup water and heat to thicken. Stir nuts and liqueur into cornstarch mixture. Allow mixture to cool. Pour cooled mixture over BabyCakes.

Jamaica Banana Topping

   2 medium bananas
   2 tablespoons lemon juice
   $1/4$ cup orange juice
   1 tablespoon cornstarch
   $1/2$ tablespoon butter
   3 tablespoons brown sugar
   $1/4$ tablespoon cinnamon
   Dash of nutmeg
   1 tablespoon rum

Slice bananas into rounds and sprinkle with lemon juice; set aside.
   Combine orange juice and cornstarch in a saucepan. Bring to a boil to thicken. Add butter, brown sugar, cinnamon, nutmeg, and rum, stirring to mix. Add bananas to mixture and poach, covered, for 1 minute on each side.
   Remove from heat and cool. Brush top of BabyCakes with orange sauce and arrange cooled bananas on top. Drizzle remaining sauce over bananas.

Toppings

Key Lime Topping

¹/₂ cup water
¹/₄ cup sugar
1 teaspoon lime juice
Peel of 1 lime in julienne strips
1 cup sliced star fruit or sliced green grapes

Mix water, sugar, and lime juice. Simmer until sugar dissolves. Add lime strips and simmer for 2 minutes. Remove from heat and allow peel to steep in liquid for 1 hour. Remove lime peel and add sliced fruit to liquid. Top BabyCakes with fruit and decorate with lime peel.

Lemon Zing Topping

¹/₄ cup lemon juice
¹/₂ cup sugar
Peel of 1 lemon in julienne strips
¹/₄ cup water
2 ¹/₂ tablespoons cornstarch
¹/₄ cup lemon pulp

Mix lemon juice and sugar. Simmer until sugar is dissolved. Add lemon peel strips and continue to simmer for 2 minutes. Mix water with cornstarch and add to lemon juice–sugar mixture, stirring until mixture thickens. Remove from heat, add lemon pulp, and cool for at least 1 hour, stirring occasionally. Top BabyCakes with lemon sauce.

Toppings

Mango Melba Topping

    ½ cup crushed raspberries
    ½ cup grenadine syrup
    4 tablespoons lemon juice
    2 tablespoons sugar
    2 teaspoons cornstarch
    1 tablespoon water
    2 sliced mangoes

Place crushed raspberries in saucepan with grenadine syrup, lemon juice, and sugar. Simmer only until sugar is dissolved. Mix cornstarch with 1 tablespoon water and add to raspberry sauce. Cook until sauce is thickened. Cool and add mango slices.

    Brush top of BabyCake with sauce, arrange mango slices on top, and drizzle remaining sauce over mangoes.

Marshmallow Meringue Topping

    2 egg whites
    ½ teaspoon cream of tartar
    5 ounces marshmallow cream

Beat egg whites, gradually adding cream of tartar. When the egg whites form peaks, begin adding marshmallow cream while continuing to beat mixture.

    You can top any of the baked BabyCakes with this meringue after they have been removed from their pans and refrigerated. (You can even top glazed fruit toppings with this meringue.) Spread mixture over the cooled cheesecakes to the edges so that a seal is formed. Then bake at 350° until lightly brown, about 15 minutes. Cool and refrigerate again.

Toppings

ORANGE TOPPING

    1/2 cup orange juice
    1/4 cup sugar
    1 tablespoon lemon juice
    1 tablespoon cornstarch
    1/4 cup water
    Peel of 1/2 orange in julienne strips
    1 large can drained mandarin orange slices

Simmer orange juice, sugar, and lemon juice until sugar is dissolved. Dissolve cornstarch in water and add to orange juice mixture; simmer only until thickened. Add orange strips and simmer for 1 additional minute. Remove from heat and add orange slices. Steep for 1 hour, stirring occasionally.

    Top BabyCakes with orange wedges, drizzle with sauce, and decorate with orange peel.

PEACH MELBA TOPPING

    1/2 cup crushed raspberries
    1/2 cup grenadine syrup
    4 tablespoons lemon juice
    2 tablespoons sugar
    2 teaspoons cornstarch
    1 tablespoon water
    2 sliced peaches

Place crushed raspberries in saucepan with grenadine syrup, lemon juice, and sugar. Simmer only until sugar is dissolved. Mix cornstarch with 1 tablespoon water and add to raspberry sauce. Cook until sauce is thickened. Cool and add peach slices.

    Brush top of BabyCake with sauce, arrange peach slices on top, and drizzle remaining sauce over peaches.

Notes